S O S PLANET EARTH

NATURE IN DANGER

Written by Mary O'Neill
Illustrated and Designed by John Bindon

Library of Congress Cataloging-in-Publication Data

O'Neill, Mary, (date)
  Nature in danger / by Mary O'Neill; illustrations by John Bindon.
    p.   cm.—(SOS planet earth)
  Summary: Discusses how the natural resources of the earth and the
living things on it are all linked together and how the natural
order of things is being continually threatened by our modern way of
life.
  ISBN 0-8167-2285-4 (lib. bdg.)   ISBN 0-8167-2286-2 (pbk.)
  1. Ecology—Juvenile literature.   2. Wildlife conservation—
Juvenile literature.   3. Conservation of natural resources—
Juvenile literature.   4. Endangered species—Juvenile literature.
[1. Ecology.   2. Wildlife conservation.   3. Conservation of natural
resources.]   I. Bindon, John, ill.   II. Title.   III. Series.
QH541.14.O54   1991
333.7'2—dc20   90-37437

Published by Troll Associates, Mahwah, New Jersey in
association with Vanwell Publishing Limited.
Copyright © 1991 by Mokum Publishing Inc.

Printed in the United States of America.

10   9   8   7   6   5   4   3   2   1

Troll Associates

About This Book...

Our planet is the only one we know of that can support life. It takes a special combination of resources to make life possible. Fresh air, sunlight, water, and rich soil are just a few of the resources plants and animals need. We are lucky to live in a world that has all of these. Our planet provides a place for billions of trees, flowers, fruits, and vegetables to grow. And it provides a home for countless animals and insects.

All of these living things are linked together. We humans are also part of the chain. We affect life on this planet with everything we do. Humans have more power to change nature than any other animal that has ever lived. These changes can be good or bad. There are many warning signs today that our way of life is doing great harm to the planet. Many plants and animals have disappeared forever. Others are in danger as they lose their homes or are invaded by people or pollution. But we don't have to let this happen.

In this book you will learn about the things that make life possible, and how plants and animals work together. You will find out about many different places where creatures make their homes. And you will see how these homes are threatened as people use up more and more space. Captain Conservation will give you some ideas about what you can do to help. Read on and find out what can be done to save nature in danger.

Contents

A Journey of Four Billion Years

Have you ever noticed how neatly your fingers are made for grasping a cup or holding a pen? Have you watched the twisting body of a cat as it drops from a high place and lands on its paws? In many ways our bodies and the cat's are like finely tuned machines, almost perfect for their jobs. Even more amazing is the way the millions of different plants and animals on earth live together. Each has a different role that in some way helps the others survive. The pieces of nature fit together like a jigsaw puzzle. Although it may look simple, nature is complex. It has taken almost four billion years to produce life as we know it today.

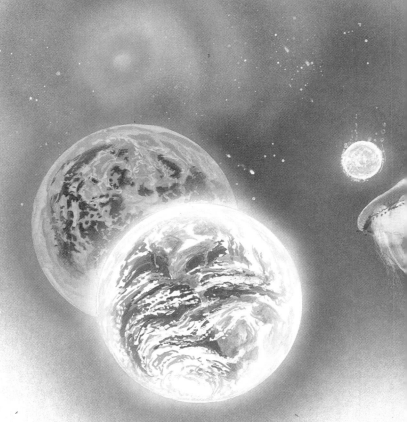

From a Single Cell ...

Earth began as a lifeless ball of dust and gases that slowly cooled to become solid. The first signs of life appeared somewhere between three and four billion years ago. These were tiny creatures made up of a single cell. A cell is the basic building block for any living plant or animal. These first living cells paved the way for all other forms of life. As they developed, they started to produce oxygen, one of the gases we breathe.

Over many millions of years, different types of plants and animals developed from these first simple cells. In the beginning most lived in the sea. Worms and jellyfish are some of the oldest animals on earth. They began to swim the oceans around 650 million years ago. Animals did not reach dry land until about 400 million years ago. These early animals were relatives of fish. They had lungs for breathing but had to return to the water to lay eggs. Animals that divide their time between land and water are amphibians. Today's newts and frogs are relatives of early amphibians.

Amphibians arrived on land to find the dry world already green with plants. The plants had also come from the oceans. Relatives of simple sea plants such as algae and seaweed developed ways of living on dry land. These new plants also grew stiff structures that allowed them to stand upright. An early amphibian would have seen mosses and giant ferns a bit like those we see in the woods today.

The Age of Dinosaurs

By the time dinosaurs arrived 225 million years ago, life was flourishing both in the seas and on land. The dinosaurs might have been the largest land creatures, but they certainly weren't the only ones. Their neighbors included smaller reptiles such as lizards, snakes, and crocodiles. Birds flew overhead during most of the dinosaurs' reign, feasting on giant insects. And small furry mammals scurried through the underbrush, keeping away from dinosaur jaws.

Besides the simple mosses and ferns, many different trees grew in the dinosaurs' world. The oldest type of tree may be a palmlike group called the cycads. These appeared around 300 million years ago and can still be found today in parts of Africa. Trees with cones, such as pines and larches, developed around the same time. Flowers and flowering trees appeared late in the Age of Dinosaurs. They added brilliant pinks, yellows, reds, and blues to the green world.

New Lords of the Land

What ended the dinosaur age is a mystery we may never solve. Sixty-five million years ago the earth suddenly changed, and dinosaurs and many other types of animals and plants disappeared. With their greatest enemies gone, the group of creatures called mammals took over. In the past fifty million years mammals have branched into hundreds of different family groups. Each group is suited to its own special way of life.

On the grassy open plains, swift-running grass-eaters developed. You would know this group today as the horse family. Their fiercest enemies were also suited to life in the open. These were giant meat-eating cats such as the saber-toothed tiger. Mammals that are familiar to us today included wolves, bears, cows, pigs, whales, and many others.

The Biggest Brains

The most successful mammals alive today began life in the trees. About twenty-six million years ago a few of these apelike creatures came down to try life on the ground. In time their descendants began to walk upright and developed larger brains. By about four million years ago some of these creatures began to resemble humans of today. They were enough like ourselves to be called hominids. This name means "humanlike."

True humans have only been around for between a quarter to a half of a million years. Although this may seem like a long time, we are late-comers to the planet. But with our large brains, we humans have the power to change our world more than any other creature that has ever lived.

The Wonderful Web of Life

It is a beautiful sight to watch a bumblebee make its way through a field of snapdragons. The bee gets nectar from the flower to make honey. But the bee is also doing the snapdragon a favor. On its hairy hind legs the bee picks up dustlike pollen from the flower and carries it to other snapdragons. Snapdragons need this pollen to reproduce, or make new flowers. By carrying the pollen, the bee helps the flowers.

Just like the bee and snapdragon, all plants and animals in nature are connected in special relationships. They do more than just supply each other with food. They may help each other reproduce or travel. Some may clean the air or water around them. Together, the plants and animals in each corner of the planet are linked together in a chain of relationships called an ecosystem. Removing just one member of an ecosystem can disturb life for the whole community.

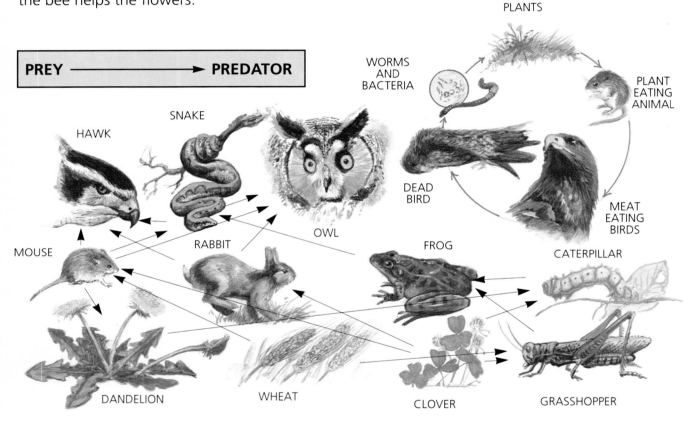

PREY ⟶ PREDATOR

PLANTS

WORMS AND BACTERIA

PLANT EATING ANIMAL

DEAD BIRD

MEAT EATING BIRDS

SNAKE

HAWK

OWL

FROG

CATERPILLAR

MOUSE

RABBIT

DANDELION

WHEAT

CLOVER

GRASSHOPPER

Food Chains and Food Webs

One type of relationship between the members of an ecosystem is the food chain. The food chain is made up of animals that eat or are eaten by other members of the chain. The first links in a food chain are the green plants. Plants take in minerals from the soil, gases from the air, and sunlight. From these simple things, they make food. When they are eaten by plant-eating animals, the plants pass on this food. Plant-eating animals, in turn, are eaten by meat-eaters. Finally, when the meat-

eaters die, their bodies are broken down by tiny creatures such as worms or bacteria. These creatures return the minerals and gases stored in the animals' bodies to the air and soil.

Of course, many different types of animals may feed on the same plant or animal. Also, a single animal may eat many types of plants or other animals. When we try to map these relationships, we get a more complex picture. It is called a food web.

Cycles of Nature

Members of an ecosystem do more than just eat and be eaten. For example, all living things play a role in balancing the different gases in the air we breathe. Plants take in a gas called carbon dioxide. They replace it with the oxygen we and other animals need to breathe. Animals, in return, take in oxygen released by plants and replace it with carbon dioxide. In this way, plants and animals keep a steady balance of gases in the air.

Water is another important part of any living community. We usually think only of the water trapped in lakes, rivers, and oceans. But water makes up part of every living thing. The air around us also carries water in the form of vapor. You can't see this water, but sometimes you can feel it as moisture on your skin. Both plants and animals need water to survive.

Plants play an important role in keeping water in an area. Their roots act like sponges, trapping water in the soil. Without plant life to protect it, topsoil may be washed away by heavy rains. Over a long time unprotected soil can dry up and become sandy desert. Besides trapping water in the soil, plants return a small amount to the air through their leaves. This helps keep a healthy balance between rain coming down and water returning to the air.

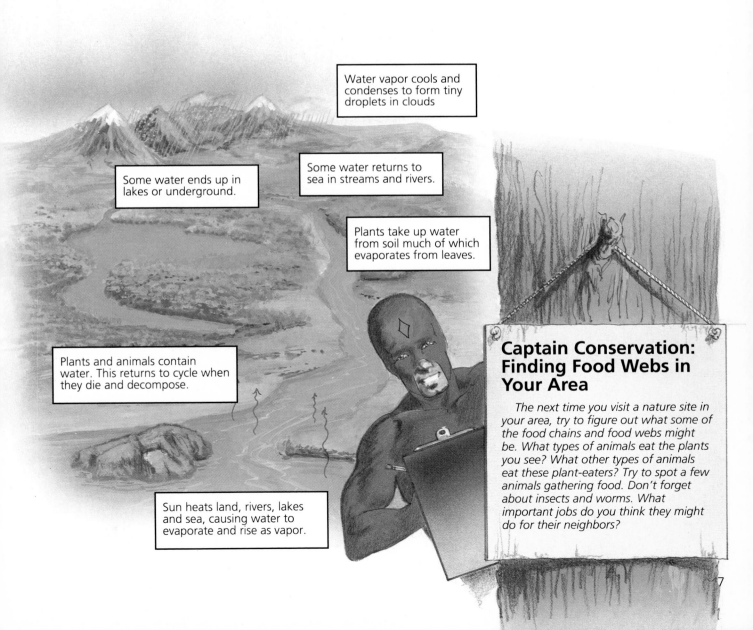

Water vapor cools and condenses to form tiny droplets in clouds

Some water ends up in lakes or underground.

Some water returns to sea in streams and rivers.

Plants take up water from soil much of which evaporates from leaves.

Plants and animals contain water. This returns to cycle when they die and decompose.

Sun heats land, rivers, lakes and sea, causing water to evaporate and rise as vapor.

Captain Conservation: Finding Food Webs in Your Area

The next time you visit a nature site in your area, try to figure out what some of the food chains and food webs might be. What types of animals eat the plants you see? What other types of animals eat these plant-eaters? Try to spot a few animals gathering food. Don't forget about insects and worms. What important jobs do you think they might do for their neighbors?

The Habitat Connection

Scanning the horizon on a clear Arctic morning, you might easily miss an amazing sight. With the sun glaring on a field of snow, a polar bear weighing 2,000 pounds (900 kilograms) might be invisible. This giant's thick white coat helps it blend into the snowy background. If you did catch sight of a polar bear, you'd probably want to "make tracks" as fast as you could! But you'd find it difficult to run through snow drifts that might reach to your hips. The polar bear can move quickly across this frozen landscape. Its huge webbed paws spread over the snow's surface to keep it from sinking.

The polar bear is adapted, or suited, to the frozen Arctic in many other ways. Its thick coat and a layer of fat keep it warm even when the temperature is minus 40 degrees. And the polar bear's diet is made up of seals and fish found in nearby waters. Like plants and animals around the world, the polar bear is designed to live in a unique type of home. We call these natural homes habitats.

Sorry—Don't Like to Travel

Animals such as the polar bear may travel far within their habitat. But life is impossible for them outside of that home. A large white bear that wandered south would quickly stand out in a leafy green forest. It would probably not eat the food there. And unlike brown bears, polar bears can't climb trees to hide from their enemies.

The plants and animals in any area have taken thousands or even millions of years to adapt to local conditions. They adapt by changing to fit into the habitat and by developing special relationships with each other. Plants and animals may also adapt to the weather in the region. Their habitat and their relationships with other creatures provide them with food, protection, warmth, and the other things they need to live. Outside their habitat, most plants and animals cannot survive for long. The greatest danger to wildlife today is the destruction of natural habitats.

Tundra

Borecel Forest

Temperate Grassland

Broad Leaved Forest

Scrub

Mountains

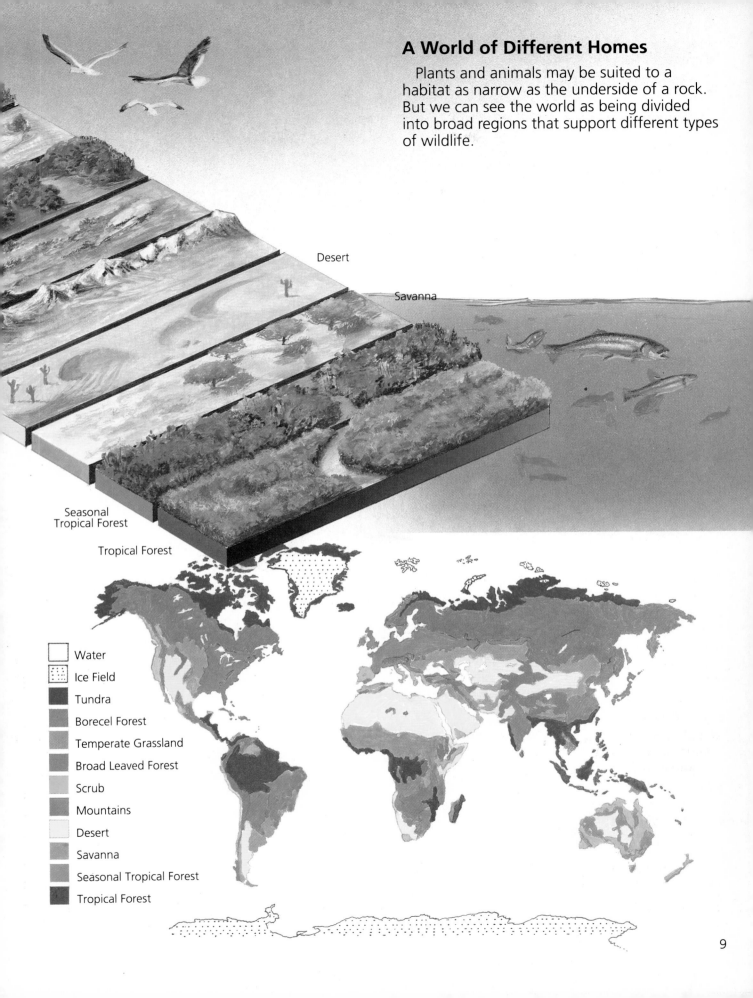

A World of Different Homes

Plants and animals may be suited to a habitat as narrow as the underside of a rock. But we can see the world as being divided into broad regions that support different types of wildlife.

Desert

Savanna

Seasonal Tropical Forest

Tropical Forest

Water

Ice Field

Tundra

Borecel Forest

Temperate Grassland

Broad Leaved Forest

Scrub

Mountains

Desert

Savanna

Seasonal Tropical Forest

Tropical Forest

Changing the Landscape

Unlike any other form of life, humans can adapt to almost any environment. Because of our gift for invention, humans can live in habitats we are not suited to by nature. We can build homes with central heating to keep us warm in the frozen north. We can irrigate deserts to grow food in dry regions.

These special talents have made human beings the most powerful and widespread species on earth. But as people move into new areas, they have a great effect on the habitat of local plants and animals. Today human activity affects all other species, even those thousands of miles from human settlements.

Clearing the Land

The most direct way to destroy local habitats is by clearing land. People clear land for many reasons: to build towns or roads, to use land for farming, or to get at oil and minerals stored under the earth. Land clearing takes away the homes of plants and animals that live in the region. As their habitat disappears, they are pushed into a smaller and smaller area. Many then die from hunger or diseases caused by overcrowding.

Pollution

People create waste in many forms. It may be solid garbage or sewage from homes, poison gases from industry smokestacks, or dangerous chemicals poured into nearby waterways. Most of these wastes end up in the local environment. Pollution can destroy entire habitats, or it may simply kill certain members of a food chain. Over time whole ecosystems can be damaged by such pollution.

Overhunting

Many of the animals that have disappeared over the last five hundred years were hunted out of existence. People once thought there was a never-ending supply of wild animals. Many animals were and still are hunted for meat, fur, oils, and other products. Today we are realizing there are limits to how much we can hunt. But it may already be too late for some rare animals. Their numbers have dropped so low that they may never bounce back.

Global Changes

Scientists are finding signs that pollution is changing the very make-up of our world. Many of the gases and chemicals we release are upsetting the natural balances that make earth a livable planet. For example, certain types of air pollution are believed to be raising the earth's temperature. They form a blanket around the earth that traps heat from the sun. Other chemicals are eating away at a layer of the atmosphere that protects earth from dangerous sun rays. In large doses these rays can harm plants and animals. Over time changes such as these may make life impossible for many animals and plants.

Shrinking Forests of the North

Hundreds of years ago vast stretches of Europe and North America were covered in forest. Wildlife in the European woodlands was so plentiful that kings and nobles used entire forests as their private hunting grounds. People on horseback chased stags and wild boars. But even these playground forests could not compare with the woodlands of 2,000 years ago. At that time Europe was blanketed by broadleaf trees. People cleared forests as farming spread out. In some places they also cut down the broadleaf trees to make room for fast-growing conifers. These softwood trees could supply more lumber for building.

In North America the forests also shrank with human settlement. Native American Indians had lived in harmony with the land for thousands of years. They only planted crops on a small scale, and the people moved often, following the herds of buffalo. The native people only hunted for as much food as they could use. In this way they caused little damage to the land and wildlife. But when large numbers of Europeans began arriving in the 1600s, they brought their land-clearing habits with them. To make way for farms and towns, they cut down great stretches of forest. They also began hunting wildlife to send back to eager buyers in Europe. Millions of animals were killed for their fur and meat, or simply for sport.

The northern forests today face a new threat. Pollution from cars and industries sends showers of acid down on lakes and forests. These acids destroy thousands of acres of woodland each year and make lake and river water unfit for plants and animals.

The Boar Bounces Back

From about the 1100s to the 1600s, the woodlands of Europe echoed with the cries of hunters on horseback. These riders carried bows and arrows and used packs of dogs to sniff out their prey. The wild boar was a favorite target. It could put up a good fight with its short tusks. So hunting boars was considered "good sport."

By the 1600s the wild boar had been hunted out of existence in Britain. By the middle of the 1800s it was gone from Switzerland as well. Only a few survivors remained near the border of Germany. But the wild boar is a fast breeder. As hunters lost interest, the boar population quickly began to grow again. A female boar has between eight and twelve babies at a time. She can also give birth as often as three times in two years.

By the mid-1970s boars had made enough of a comeback in Switzerland to pester local villagers. They were "making pigs of themselves" on newly planted corn crops!

No Love for the Wolf

The wolves of North America have not been as lucky as Europe's wild boars. They have lost most of their forest homes to farms and cattle ranches. In order to survive, starving wolves sometimes prey on the livestock that has taken their place. This has earned them the hatred of farmers and ranchers. So red wolves and gray wolves have been heavily hunted. The only living red wolves are those in captivity. In Texas, gray wolves have been almost wiped out by ranchers.

Red Wolf

Gray Wolf

A Royal Price Tag on Its Head

The beaver, which is plentiful today in North American rivers, was once almost hunted to extinction. A great demand for beaver fur was what opened up great sections of North America. From the 1500s to the 1800s, beaver-fur hats were very popular. Beavers had almost disappeared by the middle of the 1800s because their pelts were so valuable. King Charles the First of England might be partly to blame. In 1638 he declared that all hats must include beaver fur!

A Rain of Pollution

For more than thirty years scientists have puzzled over the mystery illness that has been killing forests in Europe and North America. In the Canadian province of Quebec, the maple sugar harvests grew smaller because the maple trees became sick. In Germany more than half of the trees are dead or dying from the effects of acid rain.

Acid rain is formed when certain types of air pollution mix with water vapor in the atmosphere. The two main causes of acid rain, sulfur dioxide and nitrogen oxide, form acids when mixed with water. These acid drops fall to earth when it rains or snows. Most nitrogen oxide comes from car exhaust fumes. Sulfur dioxide comes mainly from industry smokestacks and power plants.

Tropical Rain Forests

South America
Brazil

Altamira

Eyewitness Report
Altamira, Brazil: March 2, 1989

A planned series of dams to be built in the dense jungle of Brazil over the next twenty years has brought together an odd collection of people from around the world. More than 600 Indians who live in the forest traveled to the city of Altamira to protest the building of the dams. They were joined by many outsiders concerned about the environment. Among them was the rock star Sting. He met with the president of Brazil to discuss raising money to save the rain forest.

As many as twenty dams may be built in the region. They could flood up to 100,000 square miles (260,000 square kilometers) of forest. Besides thousands of plant and animal species found nowhere else in the world, the Amazon jungle is home to more than 200,000 native people.

An Undiscovered World

Losing our tropical forest is one of the greatest threats to wildlife on earth. Rain forests cover nearly one tenth of the planet's surface. Yet scientists know little about life in these jungles. We do know that two fifths of all species live in the rain forest. Many of these are plants and animals that have not even been discovered yet!

As well as being home to nearly half of life on earth, rain forests play an important role in keeping our air clean. Covering millions of acres, these huge forests produce much of the oxygen people and animals need to breathe. Rain forests also take thousands of tons of carbon dioxide out of the air. Scientists fear that too much carbon dioxide in the atmosphere is causing our planet to overheat.

Flames and Chain Saws

Each year 124,000 square miles (320,000 square kilometers) of rain forests disappear. Trees that have taken hundreds of years to grow are cleared in a matter of hours. They are destroyed by chain saws, bulldozers, fires, or flooding. If we continue to clear rain forests at this speed, they could be gone by around the year 2030.

Why do we cut down these forests if we know they are so valuable? Many of the countries where rain forests grow are poor. They owe large amounts of money to international banks and other countries. Many of the cities in these nations are also overcrowded. By cutting down forests, people hope to develop land for cattle, lumber, and farming. Forest land can also be destroyed by flooding when huge dams are built for electricity. These projects are aimed at earning money so people can live. As long as these countries are in debt, they will probably continue to chop down trees. People around the world are looking for ways to help these nations find other ways to fight poverty.

Swapping Debt for Forest

Some organizations are trying to help poor countries out of this difficult corner. They offer to "buy" some of the debt owed by these countries. This means that they pay the money owed to the bank. In return, they ask the nation to protect part of their forests for wildlife. These organizations depend on money donated by ordinary people.

The Old Man of the Forest

As the rain forests of Borneo and Sumatra in Southeast Asia disappear, we may lose one of the most intelligent members of the ape family. The fat cheeks and red beard of the male orangutan have earned it the nickname "old man of the forest." Orangutans are fruit-eaters. In their jungle home they often have to travel far to find fruit trees. But as local rain forests are cut down to make room for plantations, the orangutans find themselves with less and less space. Soon we may see this swinging ape only in zoos.

At Home Only in Your Home

It's hard to believe, but one of the rarest flowers in the wild is a plant we see almost every day. The African violet, Saintpaulia ionantha, is a favorite house plant. But in its native home in the hillside forests of Tanzania, these violets have almost disappeared.

Life on the Coasts

Around the world the shoreline where ocean and dry land meet provides a special home for thousands of plants and animals. The coastlines that fringe each continent are year-round homes for some animals. For others they are a place to visit for feeding or laying eggs. In addition, the rich plant life of the coasts does important jobs by cleaning the water of some pollution and protecting the land from the pounding of wind and waves. The coastal frontier is also a barrier that protects inland areas from salty ocean water.

Many different ecosystems make up the coastlines of the world. In warm regions mangrove forests and coral reefs may rim the land. Cooler salt marshes are more common in northern countries. All of these ecosystems are in danger from human development. Two thirds of all the people on earth live along just one third of its coastline. Much of the coastal land has been cleared to make way for cities, farms, and highways, or for use as garbage dumps. Life along the coasts and river mouths is also threatened by sewage and other pollution poured into the waters.

The Noise Makers of San Francisco

At low tide the salt marshes of San Francisco Bay in California are filled with noisy birds hunting for snails as well as fiddler crabs and other shellfish. The noise is not as loud as it once was, however. Local pollution has made feeding in the area dangerous for these birds, called clapper rails. A few decades ago their numbers dropped as female clapper rails laid eggs with shells too thin to protect the young inside. Scientists found that a pesticide called DDT was to blame. This pest-killing chemical got into the clapper rails' food and poisoned the birds. DDT use has been banned in the United States since 1972. This gives the birds a fighting chance. But today they are still an endangered species.

Clapper Rail

Captain Conservation: Keeping the Waters Clean

You can do your part to protect coastline wildlife. Don't use your drains as a garbage dump. Many liquids used at home, such as cleaners, paint, and pest-killing chemicals, are poisonous to wildlife. Poured down your drain, they may find their way into nearby waterways. Added to poisons from thousands of other sources, they can kill animals and plants in their coastal homes. Find out safe means offered by your town or city for disposing of these harmful fluids.

Saltwater Forests of the South

Bordering the warm countries near the earth's equator are strange trees that seem to stand on stilts. Their "stilts" are actually long prop roots that hold the trees above water. These swamp trees are called mangroves. Mangrove forests are home to many species of animals that supply humans with food, especially fish and shellfish such as shrimp. The trees' strong roots also hold on to the soft, sandy soil that might be washed away by the pounding of the ocean.

In spite of the important jobs they do, mangrove forests are being destroyed. More than one third of the mangroves have already disappeared. Mangrove forests are cut down to use as fuel or to make way for farming. As the mangroves disappear, scientists estimate that twenty types of plants and nearly ninety animal species may lose their homes.

Crocodile in Danger!

This toothy fellow, the estuarine crocodile, makes his home in mangrove forests and river deltas of Asia and Australia. The estuarine crocodile faces danger as its home is chopped down and burned. But its attractive skin causes it problems, too. Crocodile skin can be sold to make shoes, handbags, and wallets. The chance to make money off its hide makes the estuarine crocodile a favorite target for hunters.

What If the Oceans Rise?

Coastal life may face the greatest danger of all over the next century. Many scientists fear that a certain type of air pollution is causing earth's temperature to rise. Carbon dioxide in the air forms a screen around the planet that traps warm rays from the sun. This trap is needed to keep earth warm enough to live on. But too much carbon dioxide in the air may be overheating the planet. This warming process is called the greenhouse effect.

Because of the greenhouse effect, some scientists predict the earth's temperature might rise as much as nine degrees Fahrenheit (five degrees Celsius) by the year 2030..The temperature change would be greatest at the North and South Poles. At the poles huge sheets of ice hold two percent of the earth's water. If higher temperatures caused this ice to melt, millions of tons of water would pour into the oceans. Ocean levels around the world might rise a few feet as a result.

Rising sea water would flood coastal areas. Millions of plants would die. Animals would have nowhere to run. They could not quickly learn to live inland even if they could reach higher ground. It takes thousands of years for species to adapt to new conditions. If water levels rise over the next fifty years, many types of plants and animals could disappear.

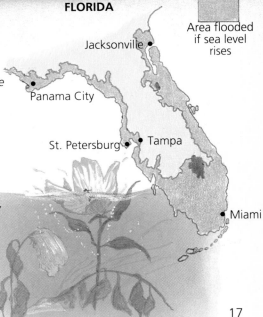

FLORIDA

Area flooded if sea level rises

Jacksonville

Panama City

St. Petersburg • Tampa

Miami

The Frozen Lands

The North Pole and South Pole of our planet seem like frozen wastelands to most of us. We usually think of both the Arctic and Antarctic as little more than huge sheets of ice. But these two poles support different forms of life and are not at all the same under the snow. The Arctic is actually a small ocean surrounded by the northern lands of North America, Europe, Greenland, and Asia. The ice that covers these chilly waters is only a few dozen yards thick. The lands that reach within the Arctic hold a surprising range of animals. Large plant-eaters such as caribou and reindeer live on the mosses, lichens, berries, and low-lying shrubs that grow in the North. Small meat-eaters such as the arctic fox chase arctic hares and lemmings. And from the broken ice floes (large, flat sections of floating ice) that fringe the Arctic Ocean, giant polar bears hunt seals and fish.

Antarctica is nearly twice as large as western Europe because of the ice that spreads far beyond the land. This ice is almost a mile and a half (almost two and a half kilometers) deep! Antarctica is surrounded by a vast ocean rich in fish and ocean mammals. Whales, fur seals, and sea gulls come to feed in these waters. The land is ruled by waddling penguins.

Both poles lie far away from large cities and most industries. Yet life in these remote areas shows signs that pollution has reached even here.

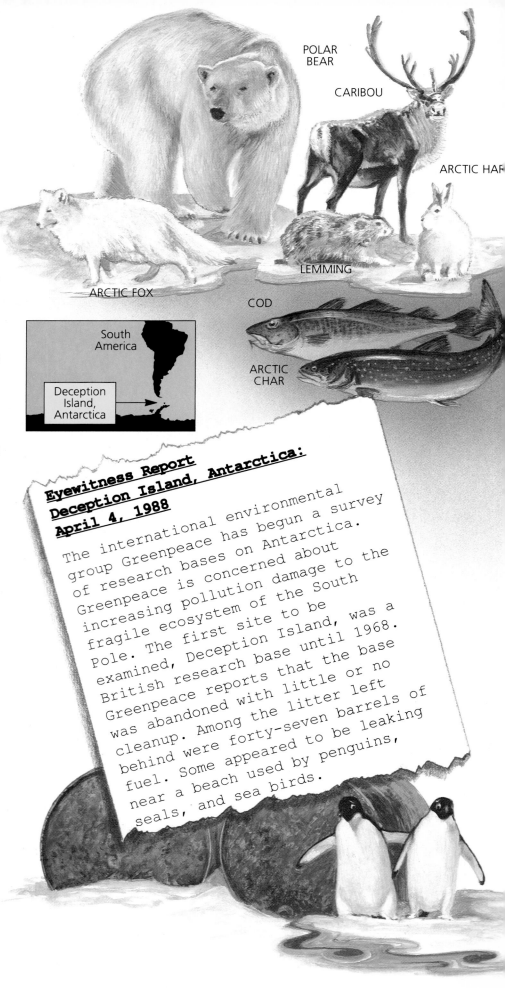

POLAR BEAR

CARIBOU

ARCTIC HAR

ARCTIC FOX

LEMMING

COD

ARCTIC CHAR

South America

Deception Island, Antarctica

Eyewitness Report
Deception Island, Antarctica:
April 4, 1988

The international environmental group Greenpeace has begun a survey of research bases on Antarctica. Greenpeace is concerned about increasing pollution damage to the fragile ecosystem of the South Pole. The first site to be examined, Deception Island, was a British research base until 1968. Greenpeace reports that the base was abandoned with little or no cleanup. Among the litter left behind were forty-seven barrels of fuel. Some appeared to be leaking near a beach used by penguins, seals, and sea birds.

HUMPBACK WHALE

PENGUIN

SPERM WHALE

FIN WHALE

ANTARCTIC FUR
SEAL

SEA
LION

KRILL

Managing the Last Frontier

The southern continent, Antarctica, is a bone-chilling land of howling winds year-round. It is also the last unspoiled continent. Decisions about the future of Antarctica are made by a number of countries acting together. Until the 1990s, only research had been done in Antarctica. No mining or drilling had taken place, although the area is thought to be rich in iron ore and oil.

The animals of Antarctica have not fared as well. Ships from several countries have nearly wiped out several types of animals over the years. In the 1800s fur seals were hunted until they nearly disappeared. Their numbers did not improve until the 1970s. In the 1930s the number of whales in the area dropped sharply. New "factory ships" allowed hunters to catch whales and remove their oil on board the ship. This meant hunting could continue at a faster pace. Fish such as cod have also been caught in such great numbers that they have been in danger at times. Today a tiny member of the Antarctic food chain is being heavily fished–krill. If too many of these shelled creatures are caught, many Antarctic animals could starve.

The Krill—Small but Precious

The oceans around the Antarctic continent are filled with krill. These little cousins of the shrimp are the most important source of food in the southern ocean. Six types of seal, eight types of whale, and more than fifty bird species live on krill. Years ago fishermen were not interested in these tiny fish. But recently krill have been heavily harvested. They are mostly used for cattle feed or ground into fertilizer.

In the mid-1980s the numbers of krill caught dropped by almost half over just one year. This was a warning that the krill might be in trouble. If their numbers continue to drop, the whole chain of Antarctic life will be affected.

The Fragile North

Humans have affected life in the North for many years. Around two million people live within the Arctic Circle. Natural gas and many types of minerals have been taken from the land and sent south. Boats come from around the world to fish in Arctic waters. And at times whales and seals have been hunted until few were left.

Pollution from the south is finding its way into Arctic food chains. Dangerous substances called PCBs have been found in the flesh of seals and polar bears. PCBs were widely used in electrical equipment in the 1960s. Since people learned about the dangers of PCBs, they are no longer produced in most countries. But the PCBs made years ago are still in the environment. They do not break down easily. PCBs can travel far in the atmosphere and then come down with rain or snow. They are first taken in by tiny plants and animals at the bottom of the food chain. As these are eaten by larger animals, the PCBs build to higher and higher levels in the body cells. Once in the body, PCBs can cause many kinds of illnesses.

19

The Underwater World

Our world is really a world of water. More than two thirds of earth's surface is covered in water. Most is held in the salty oceans. Yet we know amazingly little about what life is like for the plants and animals that make up this watery kingdom.

For a long time humans have thought of the oceans as bottomless dumping grounds. The vast stretches of water seemed able to swallow whatever we poured in. The oceans have also been a great source of food. We harvest fish, birds, and mammals from them. With modern technology we are also drilling deep under the oceans for oil and gas. To bring these resources back to land, thousands of gallons of fuel are carried in huge tankers. As these ships sail the oceans, they sometimes lose all or part of their cargo. These oil spills can have deadly effects on life in the waters.

As we learn more about life in the oceans, we find that humans have affected them more than we once thought. Signals from ocean life tell us that these waters might not be able to stand much more abuse.

Victims of the Hunt

As far back as the 1100s, an ocean giant called the right whale was the favorite catch of French and Spanish whalers. This creature got its name because, being fat, slow, and rich in valuable whale oil, it was the "right" catch!

Until the end of the 1800s, right whales were plentiful in the waters off North and South America and Europe. But in 1901 a new way was found to improve the flavor of whale oil. This meant the oil could be added to foods. The hunt for whales then reached its peak. Soon the right whales and their cousins, the blue whales and humpback whales, were nearly wiped out.

Whales have continued to be hunted through the twentieth century. As one species becomes rare, a new type of whale is hunted. In 1985 an agency called the International Whaling Commission began a five-year ban on all commercial whaling. But since the commission has no power to prevent whaling, the hunt goes on.

A Watery Wasteland

Probably the greatest threat to oceans today comes from huge sewage pipes. These pipes dump thousands of tons of waste into the waters each day. This chemical soup carries fertilizers and pesticides that have run off farm land, oils and heavy metals from industry, and cleaners and other chemicals from household sewage. And since nuclear power arrived, radioactive wastes make their way to the ocean, too.

United Kingdom

Sellafield •

Eyewitness Report
London, England: December 15, 1983

Britain's largest nuclear-fuel reprocessing plant is about to get a cleanup job that will cost 150 million pounds (250 million dollars), according to management. British Nuclear Fuels Limited stated that the money will be spent to lower the amount of radioactive waste discharged from the Sellafield nuclear complex.

Sellafield has been the site of unusually high levels of radioactive spills. It is believed that somewhere between one-quarter to one-half ton of plutonium has been released into the Irish Sea. The new money will not stop the discharge completely, but will lower its levels.

Cleaning Up the Seas

Countries around the world can see there is a limit to the waste that can be dumped into the sea. Several nations work together through the United Nations Environmental Program (UNEP). UNEP has launched cleanup zones in several parts of the ocean. They are modeled on the successful cleanup of the Mediterranean Sea.

In 1976 seventeen Mediterranean countries signed an agreement that they would work together to clean up their troubled waters. Since that time, they have taken many direct steps to stop pollution and save endangered species. More than eighty ocean laboratories watch for pollution in the area. And special areas have been set aside to protect Mediterranean sea animals. These include the sea turtles around Turkey and Cyprus, and monk seals off the island of Crete. Many people hope the cooperation to save these waters can be repeated around the world.

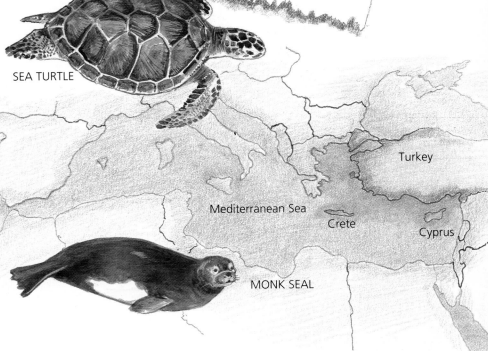

SEA TURTLE

Turkey

Mediterranean Sea

Crete

Cyprus

MONK SEAL

21

On the African Plains

The sweeping grasslands of East Africa hold an exotic mix of wild animals. The semidry savanna with its yearly dry season is home to only a few plant types. But it supports more wild mammals than any other environment on earth. This bloom of life is possible because of special relationships between animals and the plants they depend on. Over millions of years, the dozens of grass-grazers and shrub-browsers of the region have become efficient at using their local food.

While Africa is rich in wildlife, it is poor in other ways. A growing population and spreading deserts often force animals and people to overuse good lands such as the savanna. Local farmers see the grasslands as new grazing areas for their cattle. But the blend of cattle and wildlife has not often worked well.

Some of the wild animals also carry a high price on their heads. Demand for animal hides, tusks, and other body parts encourages poachers (hunters who kill animals protected by law). Poaching can make it difficult to save wild animals.

The Deadly Cost of Ivory

For thousands of years, people have worn earrings, necklaces, rings, and bracelets made from ivory. This smooth white substance can be carved into many beautiful shapes. Ivory comes from the tusks and teeth of many kinds of animals. It is because of their valuable tusks that African elephants are in danger from poachers.

In the 1980s poaching caused the population of African elephants to drop by half. Hunters shoot elephants with high-powered rifles. Then the tusks are removed with axes and chain saws. Often, their huge bodies are just left behind. There are thought to be fewer than half a million elephants left in Africa. One African country, Kenya, has lost more than two thirds of its elephants. Kenya relies heavily on money from tourists who come to see its wildlife. So while the surviving elephants roam Kenya's parklands, the skies buzz with small airplanes. These planes keep an eye out for hiding poachers. Game wardens below have orders to shoot illegal hunters on sight.

With these strict measures, the hunt for the African elephant seems to be slowing. But like all wild game in Africa, the elephants may suffer in the long term as their habitat becomes smaller and smaller.

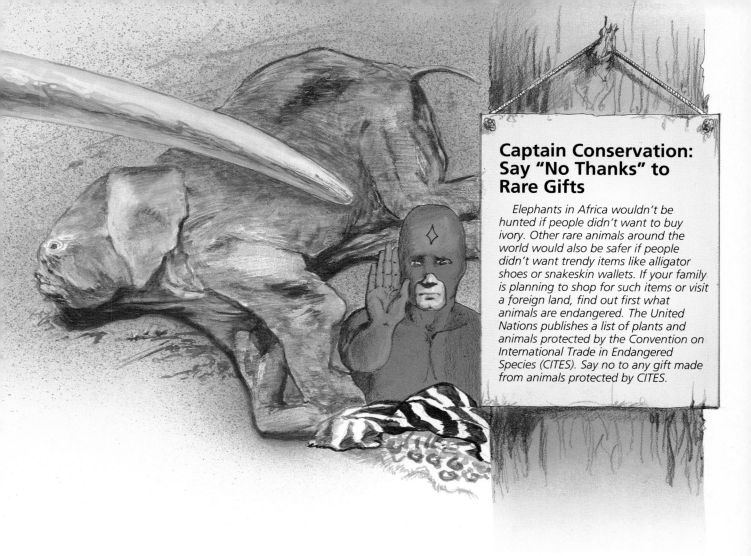

Competing With Neighbors

An African elephant eats over 300 pounds (135 kilograms) of food a day. At this rate a herd can quickly strip an area of grassland. So elephants must keep moving over a wide area. In the past the cattle herders of Africa also kept moving. They allowed their animals to roam over a large area. Domestic animals such as cows are more particular about their food than wild grazers such as wildebeests, zebras, and gazelles. Once domestic cattle move into an area, they eat only their favorite grasses. This leaves weedy plants free to take over. Within a few years entire areas of grassland can be ruined for wildlife that has lived there thousands of years.

If they keep moving, wild animals do not strip the land. But today both wildlife and people are tied down to fixed areas. The wildlife is confined to national parks. The herders can use only the land outside these limits. Relations between the herders and wildlife are not always friendly.

Keeping large animals in a small area brings other problems. Trees and grass that have been grazed have little chance to regrow before being eaten again. Large animals like elephants can strip trees bare. This changes the habitat, making it unlivable for other animals.

Changes Down on the Farm

Life on the farm has come a long way. In many countries today farms are no longer the colorful patchwork of little fields they once were. Instead, huge fields of a single crop stretch as far as the eye can see. With fewer crops spread over a wide area, farmers can harvest and plant with the help of machines. Fewer crops also mean buying fewer types of seeds, fertilizers, and pesticides. Not many farmers today try to raise a mix of meat, grains, and vegetables to feed themselves. They focus on one or two crops that can be sold for cash.

Modern science has allowed us to change the way plants and animals live and grow. Many cattle and crops have become so dependent on us that they can't survive without human help. Many seeds today need fertilizers and pesticides to survive. Some cattle are too defenseless to live in the wild. They also need vaccine shots to protect them from disease.

In the ten thousand years since people began to farm, we have chosen to raise only a few of the possible plants and animals. These few types have been interbred (combined with each other) for so long that they have little natural resistance to pests and disease. Great numbers of such plants and animals can be wiped out by a single pest.

A Green Revolution

Early in the 1960s the countries of the United Nations were worried about hunger in the world. Each year millions of people were starving to death. To combat hunger, these nations proposed a huge increase in food production. The battle against hunger was to be fought with new "super" grains. These grains were specially bred to grow quickly and produce greater harvests. They are known as high-yield varieties (HYVs).

HYVs quickly impressed farmers around the world. Instead of just two crops per year, the same land could grow three crops. Poor countries such as India and the Philippines changed over from traditional seeds to the new super grains. Their harvests quickly increased. This raised hopes that world hunger could be beaten.

The Chemical Cost

More than twenty years after the start of the Green Revolution, people around the world continued to starve. Where had the plan gone wrong?

One thing most countries did not expect was the great amount of money they would have to spend on chemicals. The high-yield varieties have to be sprayed with large doses of pesticides. They have little protection against insects and other pests. The problem is made worse when the same crop is planted over huge tracts of land. If a pest strikes, an entire region can be wiped out. In smaller mixed-crop farms, only part of the crop fails. This is because pests are quite fussy about the type of plant they attack.

The new grains also demanded a lot of fertilizer. India was one country that showed great improvement in its harvests by using HYVs. Over a twenty-year period wheat harvests increased by fifty percent. Rice harvests were up twenty-five percent. But in the same period fertilizer use grew by an amazing two thousand percent!

Only countries that could afford to spend money on these chemicals have shown great results from using HYVs. This means that the poorest countries have stayed poor.

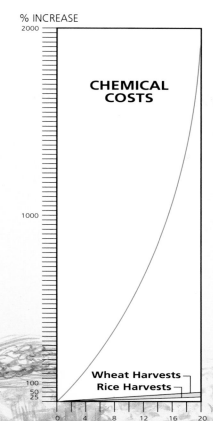

% INCREASE

CHEMICAL COSTS

2000

1000

100
50
25

Wheat Harvests
Rice Harvests

0   4   8   12   16   20
YEARS

Playing With Nature

While some chemical companies change the outsides of seeds, some scientists are changing the insides of seeds. The growth of all living things is controlled by codes written into each living cell. These codes are contained on things called genes. Each gene is responsible for a different characteristic. If you have blue eyes, for example, your body cells must carry a gene for blue eyes.

Scientists try to "improve" certain types of plants and animals by adding new genes. If a gene from one kind of organism would be useful to another, they try to add it on. This process is called genetic engineering. Through genetic engineering, scientists hope to make crops that can fight off pests, survive cold and drought, or even make their own fertilizers.

Some people worry about the effects genetically engineered plants and animals might have. How will plants and animals that have grown side by side for millions of years deal with these new neighbors?

A Package Deal

Today's seeds are more than just seeds. Most are coated with a range of chemicals. These act as fertilizers and pesticides. But some are even designed to protect the seed against other chemicals! Many seed companies are owned by large chemical companies. Seeds that depend on their chemicals are more profitable to these companies. But they mean higher costs for farmers and more chemicals on the food we eat.

Our Limited Food Basket

We actually eat only a tiny fraction of the food earth offers. Around 80,000 plants could be eaten. Yet we grow only about 150 of them on a wide scale. Only eight plants make up three quarters of the food we eat. Wheat, maize, rice, and potatoes make up most of our diet. We also eat only a few kinds of animals. Today 118 types of cattle are dying out in Europe and the Mediterranean region. Only thirty types are actively bred.

Gifts From the Wild

Most of the food we raise today developed from wild ancestors. Even now a domestic breed might be combined with a wild cousin to make it stronger. We use only a tiny part of nature's wealth. But it is important to preserve a rich variety of wild plants and animals. Insects and other pests can wipe out an entire species if all its members are the same. Variety is the key to survival.

Nature provides us with much more than food. Clothing is made from natural fibers such as cotton or silk. More than forty percent of our medicine also comes from the wild. Often these benefits are discovered almost too late. As wild lands around the world disappear, we may lose forever plants and animals that could solve many of our problems. These two pages hold just a few of the many surprising gifts nature has given us.

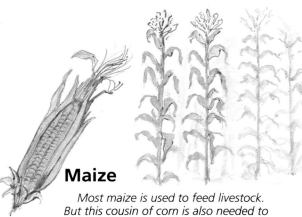

Maize

Most maize is used to feed livestock. But this cousin of corn is also needed to make an amazing variety of things. It goes into plastics, paper, tires, and the medicines aspirin and penicillin.

Rosy Periwinkle

Thanks to a flower found in the tropical forest of Madagascar, many children with the blood disease leukemia can lead a normal life. Not long ago this disease killed most of its victims—mainly children. But a drug made from the rosy periwinkle greatly increases their chances of survival.

Foxglove

The common foxglove plant has helped millions of people with heart trouble. The drugs digoxin and digitalis are made from this plant. They help to stimulate weak hearts.

Manatee

Very few of these sea mammals survive in North American waters. But researchers think at least one type of manatee may be able to solve some mysteries about a rare blood disease called hemophilia. People who suffer from this disease have blood that will not clot. This means that they can bleed to death from simple cuts or bruises. A type of manatee found in the waters off North America has slow-clotting blood. By studying these creatures, scientists hope to find a cure for hemophilia.

Investing in a Gene Bank?

To protect the world's wild treasures, many countries have begun to save seeds and cuttings from their native plants. The seeds and cuttings are stored in a "gene bank" where they can be kept for later use. As wild lands disappear, so do thousands of species of plants that might bring great benefits someday. Seeds properly stored can be saved for many years. Later they can be bred with domestic crops as needed.

But seeds stored away from their habitat lose touch with natural conditions. They are not able to fight off new pests that may develop in the wild. Many people feel that "gene parks" would be far better than gene banks. These would be large areas simply allowed to grow wild. Native plants and native pests could continue the battles they have waged for thousands of years. This would ensure a healthy active supply of plant genes. These genes could help crops cope with natural enemies. But space is tight. Many countries have no room for "gene parks" as they struggle to feed their people.

Aloe Vera

Chances are that if you buy shampoo, suntan lotion, or lip balm, it may well contain aloe vera. This spiny plant does well in dry regions such as parts of Spain and California. It produces a substance that protects the plant—and our skin—from the drying rays of the sun.

Guayule

The main source of natural rubber is the rubber plantations of Asia and South America. These trees are all grown from a small stock of related plants. Attacks by fungus and other pests have some people worried about our supply of natural rubber. A wild shrub called guayule may be the answer. This desert plant produces a gummy sap that makes natural rubber.

Captain Conservation: Be a Wild Gardener!

If your family has a garden, try letting a little of it go natural. You'll learn a lot about wild grasses and flowers in your area. You might also find some fascinating insects, birds, frogs, and toads coming to visit.

Wilderness Safe Zones Around the World

The story of endangered wildlife is not all doom and gloom. Several species thought to be nearly gone have been saved in the past century. One of the greatest steps forward has been the creation of wildlife refuges. Many countries have set aside large stretches of land as safe places for plants and animals. Some species have even been moved back into areas they disappeared from long ago.

On these two pages you'll find just a few of the safe spots where wildlife gets a helping hand.

North America

Banff National Park, Alberta, Canada

The spectacular mountains of this park hold sure-footed mountain goats and bighorn sheep. Grizzly bears also stalk the highland forests.

Yellowstone National Park, Wyoming, U.S.A.

Elk, bison, and grizzly bears are just a few of the animals that roam the forests of Yellowstone. Hot springs and shooting water geysers are some of the most unusual features of this park.

Denali National Park, Alaska, U.S.A.

This northern park is built around Mount McKinley, the highest peak in North America. Nearby forests and marshes hold grizzly bears, caribou, moose, wolves, and lynxes. One hundred and thirty types of birds visit the park each summer.

Everglades National Park, Florida, U.S.A.

Many endangered species make their homes in the swamps and coastal waters of the Everglades. Among them are sea turtles, manatees, and crocodiles. Inland are alligators and white-tailed deer. More than 300 types of birds have been spotted in the park.

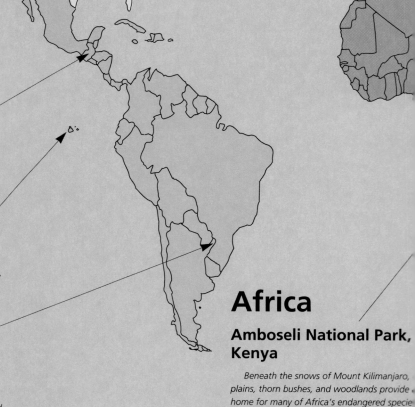

Central and South America

Tikal National Park, Guatemala

One of the earliest wildlife reserves in Central America, Tikal surrounds an ancient Mayan city. The dense jungle holds spider monkeys, brocket deer, and cat relatives such as jaguars and pumas.

Galapagos National Park, Ecuador

The Galapagos chain of islands was made famous by the naturalist Charles Darwin. The islands hold types of animals found nowhere else on earth. They have developed over millions of years in isolation.

Iguazú National Park, Argentina
Iguacu National Park, Brazil

The parkland shared between these two countries centers on a beautiful waterfall. The falls are surrounded by lush tropical forests. They hold macaws, parrots, toucans, and many other tropical birds.

Africa

Amboseli National Park, Kenya

Beneath the snows of Mount Kilimanjaro, plains, thorn bushes, and woodlands provide home for many of Africa's endangered species. Black rhinoceroses and cheetahs can be found can more common plains animals such as elep zebras, antelopes, giraffes, and lions. The rese also holds fifty hunting birds.

Europe

La Vanoise National Park, France

Nestled in the French Alps, La Vanoise offers hiking trails through the Alpine mountains. It also holds mountain species such as the golden eagle and the ibex, a distant cousin of the goat.

Bavarian Forest National Park, Germany

This highland park in southeastern Germany is a great place both for hiking and for nature study. Visitors may see red deer, martens, badgers, and some of Germany's last otters.

Minsmere Bird Reserve, England

This coastal reserve offers a range of habitats for birds. More than 250 species visit its marshes, woods, heaths, and hedges.

Rondane National Park, Norway

Wild reindeer can be found in the northern end of this park. Musk oxen imported from Canada also now make their home here.

Bialowiezu National Park, Poland

This is the last stand of Europe's most ancient forests. Bison, which once roamed the continent, have been brought back to Bialowiezu. They now number in the thousands.

Asia

Kanha National Park, India

In the central highlands of India, Kanha holds rare animals such as tigers, sloth bears, and Indian swamp deer called barasingha.

Royal Chitwan National Park, Nepal

Royal Chitwan shows off the lowland animals of this mountainous country. Tigers, leopards, wild oxen, and several types of deer roam the parkland. The waters of the Narayaim River hold two types of crocodile and an unusual freshwater dolphin.

Australia and New Zealand

Fiordland National Park, New Zealand

New Zealand is known for its rare birds. Among others, Fiordland holds a large ground parrot called the kakapo and a wattled crow called the kokako, which was once thought to be extinct.

Phillip Island Reserves, Australia

Just off the southern coast of Australia, Phillip Island holds Australia's largest penguin colony. The fairy penguin is Australia's only native penguin. These tiny birds stand just over a foot (30 centimeters) tall.

Green Island National Park, Australia

Eighteen miles (twenty-nine kilometers) off the coast, Green Island is a launch pad for trips to the Great Barrier Reef. Glass-bottomed boats offer a stunning view of underwater coral gardens.

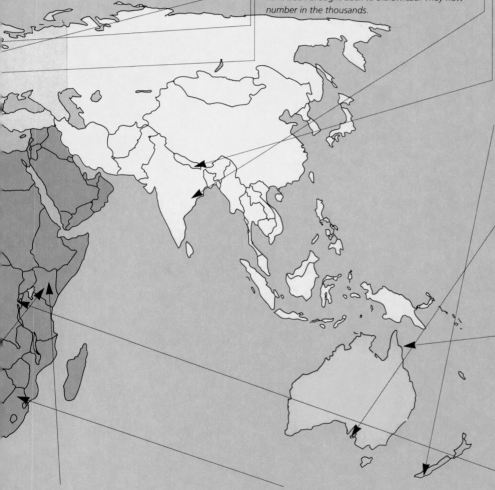

akuru National Park, enya

Lake Nakuru attracts some 370 different bird ecies. At times nearly half the flamingos in the rld can be found within this park.

Kruger National Park, South Africa

This park is thought to hold more bird and animal species than any other park in the world. It includes rare species such as the leopard, cheetah, and white rhinoceros.

Virunga National Park, Zaire

Covering more than 3,000 square miles (7,800 square kilometers), Virunga features a startling range of habitats. Lakes, rivers, grasslands, snowcapped mountains, and even live volcanoes can be seen. Dead volcanoes in nearby Kahuzil Biega Park shelter rare mountain gorillas.

Doing Our Share for Wildlife

We can't all build a wildlife refuge in our backyard. But there are many ways we can help protect our environment for the plants and animals that live in it. As you now know, pollution, overhunting, and destruction of animal habitats are the biggest threats to wildlife. You can help by not polluting and by handling nature gently when you visit the outdoors. Here are a few things you can do to make life easier for your outdoor "neighbors."

* Try to waste as little as possible. Most of the steps needed to make the things we use add pollution to the environment. The things we throw away also have to go somewhere. The garbage may end up robbing space from wildlife. Or the waste might go up in smoke, causing more air pollution.

* When you visit nature sites, treat plants and animals with respect. Don't pick wildflowers or disturb birds' nests. If you spot small creatures, watch them from a distance. If you want a souvenir, take a picture. Bringing home dead plants, birds, or other animals is a sad way to remember a happy visit.

* Find out as much as you can about wildlife in your area. Are any plants and animals in danger? If so, maybe you can help a local group protect these species.

* Find out about organizations that support wildlife protection. There are many such groups around the world. Some focus on a single habitat or species. Others, such as World Wildlife Fund and Greenpeace, work to improve the whole environment. You can help these groups by giving money, helping to raise funds, or even handing out newsletters. Call or write to a local office to see what help they need. And while you're at it, ask them for more information about what else you can do to preserve and protect nature. They'll be glad to help you. Remember, we're all in this together.

Index